WAXING THE DENTS

WAXING THE DENTS

Daniel Edward Moore

Brick Road Poetry Press
www.brickroadpoetrypress.com

Table of Contents

Boundaries bleed in pleasure's war
against the domination of reason.

Eschatology

Even though you can take me any way you want,
you've chosen to take me seriously, with teeth
in my skin reminding me why boundaries
bleed in pleasure's war against the domination
of reason, why permeable shifts between then
& now means the sheets will be changed
before dawn, before the sun spreads her
legs giving birth to a world where the first thing
I feel is the breath of God on my back.

Watching you sleep, like the *Book of Hours*
resting on the lap of God, this ring I wear,
wears me now. It's the first time it happened,
the last time it will. The first time love
ever sounded like monks breaking bread
on an altar of flesh. The last time you'll turn
from a dreamless wall and not find me dreaming
of you. Everything's pure eschatology, darling,
the old fulfilled by the new. That's why I'm
here on our first Christmas morning picking
the straw from your hair.

The Mercy Effect

One could say, you
have a mercy effect
on the hurricane that is me,
the skies' need for light
on a black whipping blue,
something yellow to frame
the bruised horizon,
a razor-sharp spike
to sew up the clouds,
so threadbare, tattered, and taken.

You're the make-up
painted on one lonely eye
staring creation to its knees,
sparks on the street
in blackout conditions,
just before rain
makes the shore of our world,
a coastline of addicts
with weak weather veins,
spinning themselves out to sea.

Magnified Darkly

In the long intermission of loneliness
        in the time it takes to put *makeup on space*

all I could do was stroke the cache,
            all I could pull were lies off my lips,

one crimson tweezer of powdered delusion
        down to the mirror, my beloved third eye,

where lifeless conditions remained untouched.
        The miraculous shadow of bed on the wall

took everything middle-aged hostage:
        first me, your fabulous fresco of failure,

a canvas stretched on an easel of light,
            then your brush, magnified darkly.

Parasympathetic Pink

Somewhere between crest and crash,
you remembered to paint the sky with relief,

a parasympathetic pink. Like the morning sweat
of fourteen years, drying on a canvas, our bodies

were chaos framed by care. When hope crumbled
into pinches of salt, into pleasure's sea of *drown*

and don't, there you stood like a lightning rod
at the edge of *swim in me*. Both of us needed

the shore to be more than a church where the sun
is praised, more than pews of emerald waves

where jellyfish sting hallelujahs. Climbing the cliff's
steps of scars from a driftwood shack of bones

made falling back down less romantic, less real,
like *Suffering* losing its paddles that night beneath

the shadow of a pearl. Holding me down,
a brush in your glass, I begged to be pink again,

to feel myself splash off the end of you like
Pollack using bourbon for blue.

Arousal Rule

Ten seconds of sleep precedes
each violation, the keys on
your spine's piano
playing wake to grief.

Drool on your pillow
is nectar from your mother;
honey wept from a buzzing womb
down the trees of her thighs.

Your choice to sleep naked
is why ghosts sharpen pencils,
a still life for the dead in honor
of the dreaming.

Memories of wake are
violently deported.
Nightmares empty pockets
to lighten the soul of joy.

Marvelous

Less marvelous, true,
lamenting my body's phallic fall.

Every night the bed became
an ice rink slashed by angel's feet;

every morning, no one's lips
had the will to open.

Remember missing marvelous,
staring at cliffs, un-climbable

for fear of the tempt to leap?
If only our bodies loved like clouds

massaging the dead with fog,
the sky could make us marvelous,

donning gloves of battered veins,
elbow length in shadows.

The Seamstress and the Tailor

I remember her trying me on, hands
      slipping through holes in my words,
            fingers dripping in adjective oil, tying

the nouns and pronouns together
      for fear they might be unwound or erased
          like so many names in the poems before
             her own walked across the page.

Thus began our obsession with fashion:
          the when to strip down and tease the light
            with every trembling violent verb,

the when to dress up and shelter the skin
      from all things cold in a stranger's eye.
             But only things that are cold.

When the sanctity of speech is threatened,
      the ten commandments on the stone of our bed
          bounce like babel with no line breaks,

an unholy syntax of *do it or else*, expecting too much
      from lovers of words. Only then do we slowly consider
         what cloth should grace the body gone silent.

Relics of the runway we are not.
         The seamstress in me and the tailor in her
           bound by garments made of trees.

We bleed paper from metaphor's marrow;
        red ink suffers the least in this world.
           Everyone knows that by now.

Eleven Hours

Darkness is nothing
if not expectation
turning its back to the light.

Rarely does the spine agree
to the fingertips' shadows, so
sheer and blue, climbing
the stairs to your mind.

Which is why when you rolled
back toward me with your hands
tied behind you, telling me
the smoke in your eyes

meant the tunnel's in flames,
I lingered there, dropped the coal
and let the engine sing.

Eleven hours
from Berlin to Paris
and nothing caught my eye,
except the smoke in yours.

Magdalene

meet me in the amen corner   be all the shouting
        this deaf man
             ever needs to hear

praise me for choosing you   my lipstick
        lord and savior
             bless your platinum

wings of hair nesting   this shameful shell
        I'll break on you
             like Joan of Arc

and cut my pain in half   a two-faced man
        with a vengeance plan
             for god to make me over

mirror me oh Magdalene   until the glass
        that holds the frame is
             crucified for shining

I am Thomas of the Tool Belt   your saint
        of de-construction
             strap me to your metal hips

seductress of detectors   and count on me
        to hold one hand
             as death manicures the other

Some Thoughts on Heaven after a Violent Storm

Tenderness remains unrivaled,
at least for now,
    when the moment is soft,
and our bodies ask
    to be held in a room
where naked we sit, quiet as
    books, wind torn pages of flesh.
Reading you as you read me,
    like tattoo gods drunk on ink,
we climb out the window
    down to the street from
where we look back
    and wave goodbye
to the chapters drowned by the rain,
    the best of us flowing
to a land somewhere with
    a library wearing our names.

Crash Site Location Confirmed

Few understand the shape
        of things, the form
                regret takes not knowing

when to say good-bye,
        even less, the feelings splayed
                like a lover's broken hand,

none of which
        fit the wind's cold glove,
                waving the heart back to hello,

back to where
        the dream went down
                as the dark night yellowed open.

Different Degrees of Radiance

A hawk hovers over the field's dying edge,
like a laying on of hands, like yours,

always, so steady, benevolent,
unlike claws fouled with flesh, more

like the calloused palms of a saint praying
the rosary of my spine.

The light's decision to shine here, too,
content with the radiance of different degrees

is why fir trees agree with a frozen sky
to stand till the ice says kneel.

The luminous, calm, daily vow
of four muddy feet on the middle path,

brings an end to the power of hungry ghosts
fed from wings of delusion. Unlike yours,

wild with deliverance, that force me
to worship the ground.

The imagination had no arms   no hands to row
the spirit home   just oars of desire   estranged from land.

Rolling DNA Dice at the Adoption Sock Hop

How I got here at all,
    after no invitation and no directions,
        after one long night of *Can't Stop* the blood

as the DNA dice on the rearview mirror
    of mama's Alabama '57 Chevy,
        danced to a violent pothole beat

over 17 years of hot tar skin,
    making her blacker than
        Methodist white, making me grayer

than a storm over Selma, the last southern
    lightning this boy's eyes would see.
        How we got there at all, with me

in the center, her hungry little crow,
    pecking the future off the faded yellow line
        as the engine of creation met the craving

of collision with the world bearing down
    on us both, where mother and son
        barely won after the game was over.

Emmanuel

Caution steered his voice at 85,
making me aware of men with sirens

looking for strangers along Highway 23
newly descended from a black winter sky

above Columbus at 10:00 PM.
My Father's latest revision of the story

of how his son must not die now,
not before the apple butter's dark brown hymn,

praises the sunrise over Minford,
not before the bed is pulled down

for the body's joy, exhausted and bound
more than ever to the mystery of a valley

known for its childhood of frog legs and saints,
and always the glory of a love found here,

called *Beauty, Ohio*, or any other name
that sounds like *God is with us.*

Right Speech

Some words should never arc
the throat's finish line flare, never
squeeze through the heart's syringe
into the needle's tongue.

The softest part concerns me now:
the name my mother used to call me
in for dinner, which in Hebrew means
god is my judge.

The blazing gavel of a Florida sun
pounded the shores of praise and blame,
over runway Number Seven before
Tampa's stars broke into tears a soldier
cried down the cheeks of my father.

Years later, an ounce of bourbon
in a copter leaving sweet Saigon made
harmful sounds into seasonal drinks,
forcing my glass to spill his pain, hot,
over ice, unmixed.

Gone Blue, Gone Gray, Gone Away

At the heart of Appalachia, near the Ohio River,
in the back of my father's throat, a combine
strips the past from the present.

Inhaling "no," exhaling "yes," everything
green and gold in between becomes rows
of what can't be forgotten.

Never have I listened so closely to the
stethoscope swinging from my soul,
or been so devoted to one man's words

beating like a snare drum in both our wrists
at the end of a battle, gone blue,
gone gray, gone away.

Made as I am of rough southern straw,
broken and bundled in muddy brown fields,
the near fatal choice of not being chosen,

is a memory none of us have. There were
no crows to scare with hands that did not
hold my own. There were no crows at all.

Blue-Collar Silence

Silence wiped his oil-stained hands
on the ragged cloth of us.
We've never been cleaner
than we are now, stripping
the gears of neighbors' names,
hearing how unburdened we are
speaking in tongues to their engine's ghost.

Blue-collar silence weighs much more
than wreckage of metal in bloom,
more than rusty handles on doors
that once burned bright for the open
and close, more than naval planes
slicing the sky into strands of protective pasta.

There's a car-seat in the yard where a bottle
of rain waits for lips to return, waits
for the mailman to drop off a box, wailing
                    with wrenches inside.

Waxing the Dents

Waxing the car with my father
always made me dream of a Hollywood prize
I would get for performing my role
with such brilliance, a script totally void of spirit,
with lots of stares and buckets of sweat.
But the prize never came.

No one outside the neighborhood knew
he rubbed it on, and I rubbed it off,
creating the delusion that father and son
found mutual joy refurbishing steel that men
in Detroit made in sweltering rooms
with masks on their tired, weary faces.

He thought the fact we'd gathered there,
under a blazing, burnt August sky,
proved we had passed that place on the road
where father and son kill each other for fun,
rather than spending a long, silent day
waxing the dents in what men made to carry
them both far away from each other.

Pain's Day at the Beach

Boy pain couldn't ask the body to stop
screaming for *help* with a tongue of sand

on a beach the shape of my mouth.
Castles were built named *harm* and *reduction*,

where adolescent pain worshipped waves
caressing my body's skin canoe, guarded by

half-naked men in chairs with pearly white teeth
blowing whistles. Man, pain made thirst into song

buried in empty bottles of glass, whiskey hymns of
know me not ever belting the sky when the spirit moved.

The imagination had no arms, no hands to row
the spirit home, just oars of desire estranged from land,

leaving infinite hours to count the gulls pecking
at my days. Speaking of the infinite, rumor has it

pain surrendered, it stopped writing prayers on third
degree skin unanswered by birds, or half naked

men or driftwood gods who found pleasure in starfish
tattooing heaven with crosses.

Mr. Big

Pain, not, a don't you dare
prayer to the power of stop.

More like reason, dreaming of a time
when the body, extremely aware,

devotes a season to testing the soul,
asking in a rippling, water board voice,

Who's in charge now, Mr. Big?
Let's see how close you can come

to the end without saying,
no, I won't sing that song.

And then the humming begins.
And then you're a child at dusk on a swing

choking the chains to heaven.
Higher, faster, don't you dare stop.

Mr. Big is so short of breath.

Dear Father Military Coma

Watching   your hands   reach for me
this boy no longer   strapped by words
spit polished   black leather   welts of love
raising the alphabet   up through my skin
no longer using   a poetics of pain   to erase
me quick   after Saigon fell
on a runway in Tampa   in eight-year-old eyes
now 60 & red   and worrying you
out of this hole   in the center of my chest
you my Lazarus   wrinkled in stone
I admit being tempted   to roll you away
then I saw your hands   not made of me
& knew I would   be you   someday.

The Architect's Son

Every boy is an architect's son.
Every son's neck is a skyscraper burning
a hole in the heaven of fathers. In time
the rain will come, but tears will only
extinguish the rage for maybe a day
that feels like a year, or until
the skin grows numb to the light
and darkness puts on a baseball glove
catching everything his mouth throws at you,
one hard word after another.

Leather is the love, you thought was a hand,
she said was a dragon's tail.
No mother in her own right mind
would dare break the architect's pencil.
Lead poisoning, God poisoning,
a rattlesnake's song humming loud in my foot.
If only the grass would have told me,
that earth is a refuge for pain,
I could have used the venom in me
to be the ink in my pen.

All the Things Your Blood Forgot
After Making You

If consolation is sonic flight in the right direction,
        comfort's a different trip completely,
attended by the falling apart.

Different as your heart in a vise at 30,000 feet.
        Different as the cabin
isn't the only thing under pressure.

Gravity is pissed, like me, at the engine's singing us home,
        home, where facts do what they do.
Except this time your name is being undone,

Grey my 21-year-old boy, in between words
        biopsy and *Monday*, beating
your future with *heart* and *failure*.

Like the wings of a plane cutting the sky into
        pastoral wrists with window seat views,
I'm inspired to take heaven hostage, to

line up the saints in 21 rows and force them
        with love to feed you forever
all the things your blood forgot after making you.

Ice Fishing

Everything warm in the alphabet died on a
hook at the end of a cold steel thought.

Some conversations have infinite holes,
frigid wounds glowing with artificial flames.

Some locations are chosen each year
to teach boys the virtue of waiting,

for quivering gills under heavy black boots,
for youth filleted and revised.

Depending on the distance from bliss,
the space between thrill and terror's next tick

determines how long the innocent stare
stays attached to god's hairy wrist, where

a tiny glass face held by two leather straps
is a metronome for his breath.

Feelings cannot afford to weigh more
than a hand on the pole. Man's hood keeps

the head bent down, halting the traffic of speech.
It takes hours for a vowel to vibrate the lips

and days for a shack where the beautiful shiver
to dream of becoming a home.

Meanwhile, I skate on the air between words.
Meanwhile, falling means nothing.

Sing, dear darkness on the face of the deep,
for the prayer of three nails and the hammer of me.

Abduction by Ponder

When the body goes on safari from the mind,
leaving behind enough food and water
to power the machinery of questions,
the cost is uniquely personal.

Anything from a ripple in the day
to a detox tsunami in your fish tank lungs,
dirty as the pupil of a shark.

Then there's the part about who shows up
when it's hopefully over, arriving dressed in heavy,
wool answers, displaying their sadness over you not
sharing a similar taste in fashion.

This is when it's good to remember
that one man's escape is another's arrival.
Nothing can stop a one-way ticket
from making the world feel safe.

Isn't this why *Ponder* does what it does,
reducing the number of candles on the cake
to the date we actually die, aversive to the voices
of fire and wax and the yearly rollcall to meltdown?

We've all been abducted by far worse things.
A last moment there is our first moment here,
blind and bound in the back seat alone,
with *Ponder* happy at the wheel.

Mudslide Boy

Of course, you didn't know. How could you?
    It's not as if you were raised like the others,
        grown from the ground of the ruptured & raptured,

the sweetly forgiven, abandoned to the truth
    of never settling down with the unsettled self,
        with words they denied & flesh they condemned

for not believing in what the hands used to call the soul,
    which turned out to be a misunderstanding;
        you thought they said soil.

The gritty, gone, going away of everything
    precious and good. A mudslide boy,
        down the hill of all your hopes and dreams,

the daily unfolding of your disappearance,
    a black & white print of your cheap silhouette,
        that an angry god fondled with guilt, while choking

on mirrors he said was the light. How painful
    swallowing must have been, & still be so wrong
        about being right, like all religions based

on blood and the million ways to spill it.
    Of course, you didn't know.
            How could you?

Fried Theology

Next to their house, in the hill's wounded side,
was a cold dark garage my Grandpa built.
In the far-left corner between shovel and hoe
stood three wooden poles crowned with sharp
metal prongs, death's summer gear for a hot
August night, when we'd wade down
the creek blinding frogs with flashlights
before they jumped into their watery world
and escape being Sunday night's dinner.
Grandma would be on the porch with her knife,
a brilliant yellow halo adorning her head,
descending from the bug light above.
She had been reading her Bible for hours,
praying our sacks would be stained with the blood
of creatures we were given dominion over,
according to *Genesis 1*. She'd always hug me
as the carving began, hoping her affection
made the carnage less brutal, less likely
to cause me any distress as we got
ready for church.

Confessions of a Pentecostal Buddhist

Baptized in the church of Pygmy rattler fangs
hanging from my foot like prayer bells in Tibet,
the water, I submit, was cold and confidential,
a lesson from the gospel of *drown me Lord quick*.
Obedient and skilled at the gestures of deliverance,
those hands knew how to shake and bring down fire.

Clouds of smoke crossed my eyes
from yards ablaze in Selma, then floated
to St. Petersburg where ash found a home.
Daddy's letters from Saigon proved a man still loved me.
I sucked the envelopes of air and kissed him
on the stamps. Mama's little boy became

a man with freckles, a buzz-cut adolescent with
apocalyptic leanings. Thinking arsenic must be
sugar's evil twin, I tried to poison her with
Sweet and Low, but only made her kinder.
Thus began my interest in pink bags with powder,
a way to live with lightning without the coming storm.

Walking on the wild side to a land of naked strangers,
this novice of the night mistook daylight for the devil.
Many years would pass before the cushion and my mind
had covert conversations about the here and now.

I remember when they started, where I was,
and what we said. It's why a candle burns
on the altar of my flesh, swaying back and forth
between the wounds and wonder.

Gospel Interrupted

Interrupting the mind can be sweet deliverance;
       every Navy Seal in me tells me this is real,
this is how little drummer boy gets to be front page news.

I want to be front page news. The best and worst of me
       splattered in red on the faces of America,
the chosen accessory of the morally confused who need

to hurt others to make sharp things shine. Does everyone
       want to be shiny and sharp, like a pedophile Baptist
choir director, or is that the way a nursery rhyme sounds

when children feel sad in their tummy? I want to feel sad
       in my tummy, a thousand miles from a preacher
with a boner, some place safer than a church selling god

on tables of wood glowing with hammers and nails.

Honor

The breath counter is watching.
The pulse police hate overtime

but love a reason to strike or reload.
Angels have no use for cameras.

Disobedience means you weren't
a match with Jehovah's DNA.

Thus, your memories made of his failures,
your beauty, her addiction to shame.

Long live hope's 10 billion stones scattered
down the hill of your body.

Long live fear's craving for light
in the dark of your voiceless name.

Be cared for, and your mind disappears.
Kindness is control with a chocolate

heart made by a diabetic god.

Elegy for Better

Most folks knew him as *Better*, son of *Never Enough*.
Born and wrapped in a denim shroud, a broken down
blue collar babe in the world of masculine monkeys
who raised their boys to excel at the game of shame
for their first birth and death for their second.

Enter Jesus, the backwoods son: his body a book on
religious repair studied in a kingdom of dirty garages
with tools that wailed like weeping mothers. And so
the boy learned to change tires like worlds with crosses
of cold, black steel, that others would hurt him with later.

In My Former Life

As a Christian assassin, Jesus gave me an eye for an eye.
Where he got his, or I got mine, neither of us knew.
There were more important things to consider, like where
to rest the recoil pad to minimize shoulder damage
and how loudly to sing the beatitudes as bullets
found homes in the Sermon on the Mount, grazing
the cheeks of troubled souls gathered to hear the carpenter
build a Kingdom of bread and wine.

Being poor in spirit, and pocket too, was all the incentive
needed to excel in the art of shattering darkness buried
below that X on your chest, no one but me could see.
If your eye causes you to sin, tear it out, it's better to be blind.
But not this man who paid the bills by trusting his
doctrinal scope and rage. I was the conductor on your
train ride to heaven, to what some call the forgiven life,
the never-be-afraid-of-your-hands-again life, the-no-fear-
of-the-sky-raining-fire-on-you life.

My job had nothing to do with umbrellas or the pyrotechnics
of mercy. For years this calling to preach the gospel *if he did it
you can too* was why I cleaned the barrel each night and washed
each bullet with water blessed by a priest who knew my name,
the name no one repeated. Those were hard and lonely days,
spent making God so happy. Standing at the edge of my grave,
would I do it all again? Probably not. The old man's been dead
for years. Endless days on the streets of gold have proven
to be disappointing. Even the angels have wings of snow.
The sun's been cold that long.

Keeper of the Hearts

For twelve hours, three nights a week,
while half the world drools on their pillows,
their eyes rolled back like filthy headlights
under the brain's dented hood; mine
are paid to stay open, alert;
to watch the strange patterns of colorful lines
fireworks exploding in the soul's eastern sky.

Crowned by technology, *Keeper of the Hearts*,
I measure the space between each crucial beat,
observing the rate, rhythm, and sound;
and how long it takes for the blood to flow
down the slopes of those atrial hills
to the plentiful fields where tomorrow is pumped
into the body's dry land.

How rare or unusual is it really,
this matter of reading the heart, to go
on safari through the cardiac kingdom,
in search of the weak and diseased?
Don't we, after all, spend much of our lives
comparing the sound of our own perfect pulse
to the terrible cadence of the world?

From history's unstable EKG, it's clear
how close to the end we are. Only a few
open vessels remain, un-damaged by previous loss.
As some of us wait, we fold our hands
into a gesture of prayer, while others deny
the pain in their chest, the line going straight off the screen.

The Visitor

On a night like tonight, Death looks like
a naked man holding one black tulip.
He offers it to me on one condition:
that I pose as a vase, a coffin,
a place where the sun can sleep on the water,
undisturbed by clouds. He feels
like the wings of a purple moth
wrapped around my body, submerging
me into night's cocoon, where I wait
for a child to punch holes in the lid
and air to fill the jar. He sounds
like thunder slapping the sky,
like monks on their knees in the dead of winter
praying to a frozen god, or
the shrieking alarms on the cardiac screen,
the last numbers pushed on the heart's jukebox.
He smells like oil on a city street
after a summer rain, technology's clean
destructive scent drifting from every gland.
He tastes like a knife dipped in honey,
causing the lips to close very gently
on what can be swallowed but not given back.

Practice Impermanence

Practice impermanence. Hold the razor tight.
It takes what it takes for each hair to fall.

Naked, on your shoulders, the top of the world,
does not need approval to shine.

It will not spin like a drunken Rumi.
It will not quake like earth's indigestion.

Something old as love is bleeding here.
The map of scars my mother drew

with mercurochrome fingers, taping light
over holes, where skin made a choice

to live somewhere else, as I, the boy,
was becoming the man she'd leave too soon to know.

Practice impermanence. Let the pen tattoo
you onto the page like grass on a bloodstained

boot, like the slain, wet whiskers of the world
on the barber shop floor of heaven.

Let the candy cane lick the sidewalk's face.
Let the door be locked. Let the comb be clean.

As the window shade says, Amen.

Psalmania

1.

As in the beginning of mathematical madness,
the part about making that's always left out.

Heaven and earth should know better,
being raised by a woman with a snake in her hand.

As in the end of psyche's first day and its
myth about fangs and forgiveness.

The tree was where her earrings slept.
The apple was always for the teacher.

2.

For the travesty made by perfect hands.
For the space between altar and pew.

Let minor chords roll down the skull of Golgotha,
spilling white lilies on Mary's cold feet.

Let major chords rise like the carpenter did, out
of reverence for wood that could hold him.

Sing, dear darkness on the face of the deep, for
the prayer of three nails and the hammer of me.

3.

When the spirit hovered over the water,
when ripples became blue-black waves

lashing the shore of a land called *Time*,
Time was protected by breath from above.

The salt on his skin was why her tongue
could not control the lashing.

Temptation is the mother of gravity.
Spirit is lust for the body forgotten.

4.

Darkness never heard the word *good*.
Separation was the key that locked them away

in places and people destined for defeat.
Breath smelled like barbeque pork, with

a noose-shaped tongue dripping mustard
and mercy for everything shiny and white.

5.

Under the wide blue tent of regret, beneath
space badly needed for divide and conquer

to cast the day into shame, stars were
a last-minute gift to the angels, making pretty

the sky for the sea. Evening is when dreams
were born to die on the second day.

6.

Jubilation appears to dominate now.
Jubilation for how the story breathes

into land and sea, the chosen domains
where all things learn dependence.

As if the joy of being made were enough
to lighten the heart's cruel cadence, even

when hunger means being eaten, when thirst is
the reason salt in your veins one day turns to sand.

Jubilation appears with teeth and fur,
scales and skin, moaning and growling,

which does not quench the need for
more to kill the hermit's pain.

7.

For billions of reasons no one knows,
dust became his special friend.

Loving it into Hollywood shapes
with dancing feet and gangster smiles,

a divine victory over rebellion,
blood red, like the fruit in a young girl's eye,

soon to fall, branch to hand, for billions of reasons
no one knows.

Feeling Tones

Who said the lonely need to find
homes for the hours nothing
inside them loves, for the minutes
in wheelchairs on long covered
porches, watching the sea's
turbulent blue wash away
memories of when they were
loved, those few and forgotten
seconds?

Someone did.

2.

What keeps me from diving into you
like a hillbilly boy at that lake in the woods
where wolves watched us undress as the stars
painted our skin with hunger?

Could it be a fear of rocks,
little castles you made at night
when the door was turned by
your father's hand?

There's a ring on my hand that is
not your father's. Focus on the hand,
not the ring. It will suffer
the passing of years,

gold breaking teeth in the mouths of wolves,
in the million ways the gallows swayed against
a future bright. There's a hillbilly boy on his
pillow tonight dreaming the rope away.

3.

When will bliss remember that craving
does not require permission to bleed before
the veins have spoken?

Conversion occurs at the level of light
on the field as body, body as sky.

Questions are doors in the crack house of heaven,
where answers grow like cancerous redwoods carried
on the backs of ants.

Mighty is the way time must be, under glass, on
the wrist of the sick and unfaithful.

So says the man: half woman, half angel.
It's like waking up with a tongue turned to stone.
My body broken for you, my shame whole as the world.

4.

Where the line break consents to the breath's revision,
the dream of restraint exhaled on the way

to untying the poem from a bed in your ear,
is that where you find me waiting and watching

to see what your mind does next? Reader beware
of low oxygen levels, of words turning blue,

hanging from trees, nooses with smiles at the end
of a story you remember hearing at bedtime.

May the wailing white space make you run
for your life, as metaphors crumble behind each step,
behind the sound of my hands in your head, turning
the page again.

5.

Why wouldn't the light be grieving
at the hour when all things fade, you included,

on the field's gold edge, turning black, then silent,
so silent it hurts?

This is dusk on the island, when the mind grows still
like a horse asleep where it stands.

Your knees bend slowly as the raptor prays
and more is revealed between claw and beak.

Should more be said about the ignorant prey, about why
the field opens its mouth, so bones have somewhere to fall?

Even shadows mourn the death of light, yours, most
of all, *Little Mustang*.

Dirty Little Poem

Daylight's dirty granular shame peppered her face
with hypertensive roses.

Petals fell to their death, claiming dominion over
roots and veins over stories of creation dependent

on failure, addicted to apples punished by teeth.
Her hand delivered transgression to the mouth.

Her hunger was complete. For every stomach in need
of something heaven could not give, for every arm

in need of strength heaven could not move, she chose
now over never. She spoke the language of ecstatic trees.

Embracing betrayal, the body decided what it could do
and not do without. No lusty landscape was worth

denying the body's belief in desire. The way it exalted
sweat over sorrow, the way it refused to sacrifice self

for a second birth fathered by guilt & attended by
unrepentant men with their godly pruning shears.

All Lips Lead to K

Was kindness even noticeable   a stranger's eyelash
stuck in your eye as the light turned green   your feet
        moved forward   into the end of days
your feet   his feet   on the world's concrete
both cracked and polished   at the same intersection
        known for its urban   shortness of breath

if only   it was that simple   if only mouths we loved
        stopped breathing on a day we said   they could
    isn't that   what everyone wants   to not be found
stretched out   like K   begging L   for one more chance
    to keep the sentence alive   you can be sure of this
        kindness is observant enough   for the naked eye to see

one body   two bodies   three billion more and god
        gives a cop   a junkie for a kid on a red-eye flight
        to nowhere and back   where all lips lead to K
K for killers immune to guilt   bullets leave   as they baptize
        the world of all things   unworthy of K
        K for kindness breeding love   in the bottom bunk

of cell 19   where prisoner 10 is born again   every Sunday
at dawn   I was nothing but a Guard whose life
        was a paycheck   spent before earned
whose wife hated me   for my love of them   wasting away
        on a row called death   with no oars and no water
beneath their boat   I was despised   for not buying a boat

she could sail away from me on   and avoid drowning   slowly
    in a sea of kindness   in a pair of shoes   whose beauty
        weighed   more than her heart   could anchor

Islands seem to take revenge on those who regard them as personal Eden's.

A Ghost Minority

Some people come to this B-movie town
for how intense simplicity feels, for what it's like
to be extras in a world, drunk on beauty,
and sad they can't be more. Down on Front Street,
restaurants and stores border the Penn Cove shore,
where not long-ago baby whales screamed
as their mothers were dragged onto boats
to live behind glass until death. But they died then,
unknown to the world, in front of a camera's glass eye.

Oh, Coupeville, I'm only one percent
of eighteen hundred minds, a ghost minority
telling the world what the majority won't.

Like why Pratt's feet in his grave point north,
to throw off the angels on judgment day when
they come for the Saints of Sunnyside.
And why he built a cabin for his boy to live in
shielding his ears from the flesh he loved
through twenty-five feet of silence.

Other unmarked historical scars are not
important now, not as important as the words
diving at me, *Islands seem to take revenge*
on those who regard them as personal Eden's.

I do not staff the Welcome Center
to a world made famous by mussels and clams,
where anyone's likely to open and close
and find something missing inside,
something smaller than a whale.

Lake Mushroom Cloud

No one swims in Lake Mushroom Cloud,
not since the lily pads ate the sun,
not since the banks of bones and dirt
rolled up their sleeves with a hallelujah fist,
and punched a black hole in the face of heaven,
a warning to those who grow weary of time,
not to order from a menu of despair,
not to be desperate to wear the lamb's blood
before the sheering begins.

For those who once thought this is how
the soul finds its way home, like
an omnicidal god with a mood disorder
deciding when enough was enough,
how shocked they were to have nowhere to strip
and lay the old body down, nowhere to soak
the sin from the bones and backstroke
into tomorrow.

If the hymn of departure is the opera of escape,
heard below the surface of Lake Mushroom Cloud,
while watching God's ashes float by, perhaps
I should at least try humming the tune,
like whistling Dixie the day we all died,
the day everything went south.

This Frost Is Not for Robert

dripping down the prairie's
                muscular back,
                      down vegetable vertebrae
wearing sequins of ice,
                sewn in rows a half mile long,
                      black as a raptor's eye.
One season closer
                to the absence of hunger.
                      Two minutes closer to fly.
This is winter's intolerance of warmth,
                of anything more
                      than a dog-tired world
unable to bark itself awake
                not here, not there, or the road
                      less traveled, no one wants to take.

Kenyon Taught Me That

The fog and I,
so gray and cold
above the field's

sea of mouths, both
agree, quietly,
beauty will stay

in bed today. Life,
fog, the
beaten prairie,

I wish it could
be otherwise.
Like the sky's

simple prayer, to
not be called
that name.
My heavens,
how could you
say such a thing?

This

The first bulb of light is slowly being
turned into a hole in the sky,
and like anything waking up from sleep,
rubbing its tired little eyes,
heaven smears its gray mascara,
down the mountains rough scarred face,
unconcerned with the wintering caused
by its preference to gaze away from the prairie
made sad by the light's abandon.

This is dawn's dangerous descent
of UV rays through the lighthouse fog,
oblivious to how it will feel in an hour
to watch its glory set the world on fire,
to find me waiting for the flowers to bend,
kissing the ground with ashen lips,
at this home, this urn, this morning.

Make Rodin Proud

The sky drips through a tube,
one drop of not knowing
who to be when not doing,
one sorrowful second at a time.

An elegant flock of Trumpeter Swans
holds my gaze on the tip of each wing,
white arms of flight wearing cufflinks of dirt
with nowhere to shine but the storm.

Married to the rain in the church of the dark,
if only the mud in the wet, black fields
could make Rodin proud,
the swans could
live on me.

Word Forest

When the house knows you're leaving it soon,
    which explains the dramatic seizures of wind,
        temperatures falling, velocity rising,

the prairie becomes a Ouija board
    crawling with fingers of Indian bones
        writing *Sad* out of mud.

Inside ghosts gather laundry lint
    for tears of the inconsolable.
        They're chewing on the check books

white receipts signed with the blue of belonging.
    Forgetting is always hardest for them,
        as memories wail from the wall's knotted pine,

as one family's voice silences others,
    the dead too weak to remind the owners
        how rare, how good, occupation can be,

if love marries time in a house by the sea,
    and something outside mortality's grasp
        is born after five years of labor.

Suffering will do what it always does
    when the wheat and chaff make a home
        in the lungs after the flames are gone.

That's what we'll remember most: the price one pays
    to burn as if the world would freeze inside you,
        the hours spent chopping wood from

a forest made of words.

Farewell Paradise Empire

To the field's black eye whose lashes of corn
                         flirted with me at dawn,
to Main Street's murmuring eighteen wheels
                         pulsing to the Port Townsend Ferry,
to the dented cushion shaped like my ass
                         holding me silent as a tombstone,
to the hardened veins of Virginia Creeper
                         bloodless on the barn's gray face,
to the frigid sea whipping castles at night
                         as I dreamt in the language of driftwood,
to the Olympic Mountains hypnotic call
                         to rise above the poor in spirit,
to the pear tree's brown arthritic hands
                         praying for morning's red glove,
to the distant symphony of Trumpeter Swans
                         making music of mud for my ears,
to the coyote's shrill of *you could die now*
                         on the prairie's acres of hunger,
to my senses dazed and vulnerable state
                         that grew soft, tender and strong,
to letting go of a world that was born through me

and refused to return unnamed.

One cat hair in a cage and all the rats stop playing.

Glass Animal

During Death's last visit to our house,
you were making jewelry out of sea glass.
One by one the necklaces came,
hanging on clouds of ball chains and leather,
dangling above a valley of cleavage,
the road between hills shattered and shimmered
with what the sea could no longer hold
in its salty mouth of sorrow.

The lighter scraped my thumbprints raw
as the dirty glass bowl of dopamine clouds
became a place where nothing lived, not even
animals a child might see. Maybe that's what
I feared the most, that you would find a piece
of me breaking through the sand, then pull
me out of a hole in your foot, howling
like an animal.

At the Corner of Heavy and Acquaintance

Somewhere, someone
        is so tired of you,
the sound of your name
        makes them heavy with acquaintance.

Heavy as in a metal jock strap
        protecting them from longing.
Heavy as in when hearing hello
        their spine becomes a cobra.

Remind me, again, why my hand
        cut a hole in your throat:
object removal, a flower vase,
        a window your heart could
escape through at night
        to teach the world a lesson?

Tenderness rarely occurs to me
        at the hour you shame the moon,
turning it yellow as a caution light,
        where you decide you can't decide
if you have the power to shine.

I wish the end were different,
        beauty blooming instead of rocks
in a grave beneath your chin,
        words falling down the stem of your neck
in the window of a store on a street we loved
        where faces stopped to listen.

The Last Bad Day of Fourteen Years

Night fell   on the last bad day   of fourteen years
a charred thumb   blistered   by a tiara of lighters
flickering out   like an Afghan sky rinsed clean
by the tears   of Midwest boys
mourning the absence   of mothers and corn
mothers who would   have prayed   for my eyes
like nuns in   the Convent   of blind yesterdays

You were   my tourniquet   my nylon savior my artist in
residence   painting air on my lungs   you are   why truth
is only a scar a place where   fingertips touch   to make
temples where relief arrives   like a foreign plane
skidding off the runway   one hour before dawn   before
the last   bowl of me   turns to dust   in the moonlight
and tomorrow chooses   to offer its life on behalf   of the
open hearts   waiting

King Erasure

At your intervention
which was nothing more
than a pageantry of Post-it notes
stained by a ballpoint's opioid ink
dangling on an inch of yellow adhesive
stuck to your armored chest,

      you told us what you wanted to be—

a cold steel coffin of pink champagne
where a jewelry box gleaming with dirty needles
floated in the hands of ladies in waiting
who no longer spread their legs like wings
sheltering veins of regal blood, as your
shimmering crown of aluminum foil
sparkled above a bath towel cape hailing you
King Erasure.

If

the best year has fallen upon us,
If we believed this was it.

If certain conditions prevailed.
If all inclinations toward harm were removed.

If the finger's need to measure the distance of flame
to skin minus night's toothless grin was gone.

If the space between lips was you, asking me
to hold my breath the way night does the sun.

If blue was my face, the sky set free
from the back of your hand's red glove.

If we burned the first day of the year,
soaking every regret in piss and gasoline.

If a matchbox coffin made for two
makes baby Jesus cry.

*I am a bucket flopping with men, a study in gasping
for air. Someone throw me back quick.*

Anti-Psalm Queer Words from
the Mouth's Deep South

Hallelujah for the still water's furious roar
pounding me like god into crumbs.
In the beginning it was want, touch, the touch of want,
being transgressed by the dangerously different,
a film noir cartoon of my body's insurrection
watching me storm through the moral checkpoint
where desire stripped down is a birdcage of beaks—
minus the shimmer of ebony wings intent on escape.
It was me who helped dirty things fly,
pigeons praying on the bed of my body
a translucent fan of origami skin thrashing heaven,
screeching listen to me, listen to hands that don't
give a damn in a stranger's pants at 2:00 AM.
Hands become bowl beneath the body of Christ
in a small southern church where folded palms
never could hold my attention. Being a member
of only one body, one sanctified torso to enter and exit,
my tongue found a reason to not swallow itself
as punishment for such incorrectness, unleashing words
like a gentle pit bull raised on the sweet meat of sameness.
Unlike David, no harp taught my hands the harmony
of sling and song. Unlike David, it wasn't Goliath
who fed me the fear of men. I was safe, sleeping there,
a conqueror's seed in my mouth.

The Catwalk

His job, he said, was to *follow me closely*
the way a cat in the frozen field

stalks the shadow of shivering breaths
measuring hunger in victim time

as fear changes contentment's eyes
from a hue of blue to unspeakable black

and claws strip tomorrow's fur off
yesterday's brittle bones.

From a nest woven tight as a drag queen's wig
the sky was seduced by a feminine hymn,

a raptor's alleluia. The holy wet his pants,
and still I was followed closely.

In the stalker's gospel of stumble and save
he watched me fall then raised me up

from the tip of the world as the runway roared
and angels applauded me bloody.

Fishers of Men

I will not cast a line, not anymore,
not when regardless of where it lands

I'm still bent on a bridge at dawn waiting
for my failures to jump.

I'm the LED bulb on the fluffer's face,
making his tackle box shine, the last

inch spinning off the rod's hot reel,
the farthest distance from feel.

Now do you see how lies take me down like
a fish belly-up on the river below?

The brighter the sun, the bigger the bottle.
Yes, he's a fisher of men, and yes, violence

is hunger with a hook, and porn technology's axe
in the ice on the frozen sea of me.

I am a bucket flopping with men, a study in gasping
for air. Someone throw me back, quick.

Boys

It sounded like
boys in the woods
kicking a dying wolf.

They called him *faggot*
and his eyes rolled to
heaven.

They called him *hungry*
and his face ate the
earth.

Like a drunk parade
of soccer ball stars,
mindless brothers

welcomed them home,
stained with the blood
of untamed things,

on a bullet train fed by
adolescent miracles no one
was asked to unmake.

A Bethlehem Morning

Two thousand years before we were born,
before Love and Death became intimate friends,
Mary took straw, dipped it in blood, then wrote
our names on the tombstone of history.

Not even her son, *The Alpha & Omega*, was
immune to Death's cellular scheme, that
violent conspiracy to weaken the walls, to
slowly disconnect the body's alarms,
preventing it from sensing a covert invasion
on the lips of a stranger or friend.

When your future is drifting down a red poisoned river
with no water, no food, and nowhere to land, all you
can do is pray. But let there be no sweet benedictions
heard from this ghostly ship. Let rage and resistance
carry your voice to the gates of a silent heaven.

Ask, "Where is the Christ of those dazzling queens,
those baby-faced men with perfect hair who could
dance away darkness forever? And what about the
angels they were given at birth, divinely appointed
to keep them from evil, who watched them die making love?"

Holy Mary, Mother of God, baptize us
in a hurricane of T-cells. Pray for us now
and at the hour of our death, whichever comes first
on a Bethlehem morning.

Wooden Tears

As in the days of Noah, fear pounded flesh
into seventy-five years of killing wood,

like you splitting my skin's pink grain,
every inch of blistered space praised the hatred of water.

The average length of one emotion
is ninety seconds long. A mouth cannot negotiate

the fear of death into words of faith
when tides eat the lungs' soft shore,

making survival an animal hymn unsung
by the tongues of men.

After seventy-five years of fear, the length
of one emotion, the world drowned

in oceans of faith. Unlike me, a splinter of light
floating up you on a raft of wooden tears.

The Fire Island Boys

Warhol wasn't the only one who loved
those Fire Island boys, marble statues
cloaked in sand, whipped by
pleasure's summer storms.

Caution fainted on a thousand zippers,
a thousand eyes and tongues. There was
no such thing as a stranger's bed.
Every mattress played the same song:

Love as if loving makes you immortal, carving
a valley of light through the shame;
the crippling years of closet-shaped posture,
breaking the spirit's spine.

Those were the days of aquatic ecstasy: steam
baths swirling with deep sea divers trading
their handfuls of pearls, risking
their lives in the dangerous caves

of some other man who had to be entered
to prove how good, how beautiful he was,
even if only for an hour. If I could weep
as loud as they laughed and rage as hard

as they loved, maybe the young wouldn't die so fast,
alone, on the edge of a viral abyss, wailing at the red
autumn moon, God waking up to the sound of his sons,
washing the sand from their eyes.

Familiar

He said,   *this is my favorite word*
          because nothing ever is   said it

like silk   in a caterpillar's dream   said it
     like praise for a   porn star's bed

for keeping him safe   honest & willing
          to live by   rules of attachment.

He used it like floss   to clean the past
     off my bleeding gums   taming the hours

loneliness made   out of whips
     & wonder.   Offering what remained

of me to test the minute's   lashing tongue
     I crushed the clock   with trembling hands

sparing us both   that wicked date
     with everything   I couldn't say.

Acknowledgments

My grateful acknowledgment to the editors of the following publications in which these poems first appeared, sometimes in earlier versions.

2 Bridges Review: "Kenyon Taught Me That"
Aji Magazine: "Ice Fishing"
Assaracus Review: "The Architect's Son."
Badlands Literary Journal: "Elegy for Better."
Birmingham Arts Journal: "Different Degrees of Radiance "
Bluestem Magazine: "The Catwalk," "Familiar"
Burningword Literary Journal: "King Erasure"
Chaffin Journal: "All Lips Lead to K"
Clackamas Literary Review: "The Last Bad Day of Fourteen Years"
Coe Review: "Lake Mushroom Cloud"
Columbia Journal of Arts and Literature: "In My Former Life"
Common Ground Review: "The Seamstress and the Tailor"
Compose Literary Journal: "Gone Blue, Gone Gray, Gone Away," "Feeling Tones"
Cream City Review: "Keeper of the Hearts"
December Magazine: "Eschatology," "Some Thoughts on Heaven after a Violent Storm"
Dewpoint: "Eleven Hours"
Fire Poetry Journal: "Blue Collar Silence"
Flint Hills Review: "This"
Glass: A Journal of Poetry: "Practice Impermanence"
Glint Literary Journal: "Emmanuel"
Ground Fresh Thursday: "Glass Animal"
Gyroscope Review: "Farewell Paradise Empire"
Hawaii Review: "Wooden Tears"
Hot Metal Bridge: "Boys"
Ithaca Lit: "Mr. Big," "Mudslide Boy," "The Mercy Effect"
Mandala: "Abduction by Ponder"

Mid-American Review: "The Visitor"
Natural Bridge: "Parasympathetic Pink"
New South: "Psalmania"
Permafrost Magazine: "Confessions of a Pentecostal Buddhist"
Prairie Winds Literary Journal: "This Frost is Not for Robert"
Rattle: "The Fire Island Boys"
Raw Journal of Arts: "Marvelous," "Magnified Darkly"
River Styx: "Fried Theology," "A Bethlehem Morning"
Scalawag Magazine: "Anti Psalm Queer Words from the Mouth's
    Deep South,"
"Gospel Interrupted"
Sheila-Na-Gig: "At the Corner of Heavy and Acquaintance"
Spoon River Poetry Review: "Waxing the Dents"
Steel Toe Review: "Making Rodin Proud"
Sweet Tree Review: "Honor," "Dear Father Military Coma."
The *American Journal of Poetry*: "If"
The *Big Windows Review*: "Fishers of Men"
The *Good Men Project*: "All the Things Your Blood Forgot After
    Making You"
The *Stillwater Review*: "Crash Site Location Confirmed"
Tule Review: "Right Speech"
WA 129 Anthology: "A Ghost Minority"
West Texas Literary Review: "Arousal Rule"
William and Mary Review: "Rolling DNA Dice at the Adoption
    Sock Hop"
Yemassee Literary Journal: "Magdalene"

Islands seem to take revenge on those who regard them as personal Eden's:
is a quote from Alastair Reid.

On this long road to somewhere, which I call "relationships," regardless of the vehicle given, dents will be made and received. Poetry is how I've learned to wax those wounded, rusty places, to own their presence by making them shine as brightly as their crash.

My unceasing gratitude for the poets whose work has influenced and mentored me in unfathomable ways, Mark Doty, Carl Phillips, Cyrus Cassells and the late Lynda Hull.

For the wisdom and compassion of fellow poets, Bill and Jan Skubi, and Kevin David LeMaster.

For artist Jas Milam and her astonishing cover image.

For the vibrant love and poetic witness of the Oak Harbor Poetry Project.

And to my children, Justin, Jenny, Caleb, Carrie, and Grey, without whom all destinations mean nothing. And my parents Emmanuel Moore Jr, Norma Jean Moore and Darlene Moore who taught me the art of driving fearless, and to make imagination my compass.

In the end it is always my beloved wife Laura, the poet, artist, lover and friend,

> *who holds me down, a brush in her glass,*
> *where I beg to be pink again,*
> *to feel myself splash off the end of you*
> *like Pollack using bourbon for blue.*

About the Author

Daniel Edward Moore is an award-winning poet whose works have appeared in many literary journals. He is also the author of the chapbooks, *Confessions of a Pentecostal Buddhist*, (Createspace) and *Boys*, (Duck Lake Books).

A native southerner, he currently lives in Oak Harbor, WA on Whidbey Island. For more information, visit his website: www.danieledwardmoore.com.

Our Mission

BRICK ROAD

POETRY PRESS

The mission of Brick Road Poetry Press is to publish and promote poetry that entertains, amuses, edifies, and surprises a wide audience of appreciative readers. We are not qualified to judge who deserves to be published, so we concentrate on publishing what we enjoy. Our preference is for poetry geared toward dramatizing the human experience in language rich with sensory image and metaphor, recognizing that poetry can be, at one and the same time, both familiar as the perspiration of daily labor and as outrageous as a carnival sideshow.

Available from Brick Road Poetry Press

BRICK ROAD
POETRY PRESS
www.brickroadpoetrypress.com

Just Drive by Robert Cooperman

The Alp at the End of My Street by Gary Leising

The Word in Edgewise by Sean M. Conrey

Household Inventory by Connie Jordan Green

Practice by Richard M. Berlin

A Meal Like That by Albert Garcia

Cracker Sonnets by Amy Wright

Things Seen by Joseph Stanton

Battle Sleep by Shannon Tate Jonas

Lauren Bacall Shares a Limousine by Susan J. Erickson

Ambushing Water by Danielle Hanson

Having and Keeping by David Watts

Assisted Living by Erin Murphy

Credo by Steve McDonald

The Deer's Bandanna by David Oates

Touring the Shadow Factory by Gary Stein

American Mythology by Raphael Kosek

Also Available from Brick Road Poetry Press

www.brickroadpoetrypress.com

Dancing on the Rim by Clela Reed

Possible Crocodiles by Barry Marks

Pain Diary by Joseph D. Reich

Otherness by M. Ayodele Heath

Drunken Robins by David Oates

Damnatio Memoriae by Michael Meyerhofer

Lotus Buffet by Rupert Fike

The Melancholy MBA by Richard Donnelly

Two-Star General by Grey Held

Chosen by Toni Thomas

Etch and Blur by Jamie Thomas

Water-Rites by Ann E. Michael

Bad Behavior by Michael Steffen

Tracing the Lines by Susanna Lang

Rising to the Rim by Carol Tyx

Treading Water with God by Veronica Badowski

Rich Man's Son by Ron Self

About the Prize

The Brick Road Poetry Prize, established in 2010, is awarded annually for the best book-length poetry manuscript. Entries are accepted August 1st through November 1st. The winner receives $1000 and publication. For details on our preferences and the complete submission guidelines, please visit our website at www.brickroadpoetrypress.com.

Winners of the Brick Road Poetry Prize

2018

Speaking Parts by Beth Ruscio

2017

Touring the Shadow Factory by Gary Stein

2016

Assisted Living by Erin Murphy

2015

Lauren Bacall Shares a Limousine by Susan J. Erickson

2014

Battle Sleep by Shannon Tate Jonas

2013

Household Inventory by Connie Jordan Green

2012

The Alp at the End of My Street by Gary Leising

2011

Bad Behavior by Michael Steffen

2010

Damnatio Memoriae by Michael Meyerhofer